Contents

Section 1:
Foundations of SQL

Introduction to SQL: Goals and Learning Path

Welcome to the world of Structured Query Language (SQL)! This powerful language lies at the heart of modern data management. Databases run our systems, from online stores to social media, hospitals to banking. SQL grants you the power to unlock valuable insights hidden within this data.

What is SQL?

- **Structured Query Language (SQL):** It's the standard tool for interacting with relational databases. Think of these databases like spreadsheets on steroids: organized, structured, and capable of holding massive amounts of information.
- **Purpose:** SQL lets you extract specific data, analyze patterns, generate reports, and make informed decisions.

Why Learn SQL?

- **Data-Driven World:** Whether you're a data analyst, developer, marketer, or just passionate about using information, SQL gives you a massive edge in understanding and extracting value from data.

- **Versatility:** It works across all major database systems (MySQL, Oracle, SQL Server, etc.), so your skills are transferable.
- **Demand:** Data-related roles requiring SQL proficiency are consistently in high demand.

Goals of This Book

This book isn't just about the 'how' but also the 'why' behind SQL. You'll learn:

- **Database Fundamentals:** How databases are organized and the language SQL uses to talk to them.
- **Core SQL Commands:** Mastering the essentials of SELECT, WHERE, ORDER BY, JOIN, and more for retrieving and manipulating data.
- **Beyond the Basics:** Advanced filtering, sorting, data transformations, and working with multiple tables.
- **Practical Applications:** Real-world examples will illustrate how to use SQL to solve business problems and glean insights.

Your Learning Path

This book guides you from zero knowledge to SQL competence. Here's a breakdown:

- **Foundations of SQL:** Understanding databases, tables, data types, and basic SQL syntax.
- **The Power of Queries:** How to ask precise questions of your data and get meaningful answers.
- **Advanced Concepts:** Dive into JOINs, data transformations, and more sophisticated techniques.

A Note on Practice

Knowledge of SQL won't stick without hands-on work. Don't just read the text; take the time to experiment:

- **DB Browser for SQLite:** In the next chapter, we'll set up this user-friendly tool to start writing queries.
- **Practice Datasets:** Look for freely available datasets online to tackle real-world challenges.

Additional Resources

These resources will supplement your learning:

- **W3Schools SQL Tutorial:** https://www.w3schools.com/sql/
- **Khan Academy Intro to SQL:** https://www.khanacademy.org/computing/computer-programming/sql
- **SQLZOO:** https://sqlzoo.net/

The Road Ahead

Get ready for a transformative journey! By the end of this book, you'll have the foundation to:

- Confidently query and analyze data from various sources.
- Create meaningful reports that illuminate patterns and trends.
- Make informed decisions backed by solid data insights.

The adventure starts here – let's dive in!

Exploring DB Browser: A Practical Tool

In the last chapter, we started our journey with a broad overview of SQL. But knowledge without practice is incomplete! This chapter introduces DB Browser for SQLite, a free and powerful tool that allows us to put our SQL skills to work.

Why DB Browser for SQLite?

- **User-Friendly:** Its intuitive interface is perfect for beginners. Instead of typing complex setup commands, we can interact directly with our database using menus and buttons.
- **Cross-Platform:** It works on Windows, macOS, and Linux, so you can practice wherever you're comfortable.
- **Lightweight:** This software keeps things simple and focused—perfect for our early focus on learning SQL.
- **Ideal for Exploration:** See the results of your queries instantly, helping you understand how SQL manipulates data.

Getting Started

1. **Download and Install:** Visit the official DB Browser for SQLite website (https://sqlitebrowser.org/) and download the appropriate version for your operating system. The installation process is straightforward.
2. **First Look:** Launching DB Browser presents a clean interface. Let's break down the key areas:
   - **Database Structure:** View the tables in your database and the structure of each.
   - **Browse Data:** Navigate through the contents of your tables in a spreadsheet-like layout.

- Execute SQL: A dedicated area for writing and executing SQL queries.

Opening a Database

There are two ways we'll approach this:

1. **Create a New Database:**
   - Go to "File" -> "New Database."
   - Give your database a name and location.
   - You'll now see a blank workspace – time to add tables and data later!
2. **Open an Existing Database:**
   - Use "File" -> "Open Database."
   - Practice Datasets: Find free sample datasets from:
     - Kaggle: https://www.kaggle.com/datasets
     - Data.gov: https://www.data.gov/

Touring DB Browser's Features

- **Database Structure Tab:** Here you can:
  - View a list of tables in your database.
  - Create new tables (we'll cover this in upcoming chapters).
  - Modify the structure of existing tables (adding/removing columns, etc.).
- **Browse Data Tab:**
  - Explore the contents of individual tables.
  - Make direct edits to values (be careful – changes get saved immediately!).
  - Search for specific records based on criteria.
- **Execute SQL Tab:** This is our primary playground:
  - Write ad-hoc SQL queries here.
  - Use the "Execute SQL" button to run and see results immediately below.
  - Build, save, and run complex queries over time.

Additional Resources

- **DB Browser for SQLite Official Documentation:**
  https://sqlitebrowser.org/dl/

Practice Makes Perfect

Throughout this book, we'll use DB Browser to try out concepts and examples. Here's some practice for this chapter:

- Find a sample SQLite database (.db or .sqlite file) online.
- Open it in DB Browser and spend time exploring the data across different tabs.
- Try writing a very simple SQL query in the "Execute SQL" tab (something like SELECT * FROM a_table_name;) to list out the contents of a table.

Getting Comfortable

Our early focus is on SQL concepts not database creation complexities. Take your time and experiment! By the end of this book, you'll be manipulating data within DB Browser like a pro!

Let's move on to understanding the heart of how SQL interacts with data – databases themselves!

Understanding Databases: The SQL Perspective - Part 1

In the last chapter, we got hands-on with DB Browser. Now, let's take a step back and understand the conceptual model behind the scenes—the world of databases from the viewpoint of SQL.

What exactly is a Database?

- **Organized Storage:** Think of a database as a super-structured filing cabinet for digital information.
- **Relational Databases:** In our SQL adventures, we focus on relational databases, where data is structured into interconnected tables. Similar to well-organized spreadsheets linked together.
- **Beyond spreadsheets:** Databases beat spreadsheets in handling *vast* amounts of data more efficiently, with safeguards to ensure data quality.

Key Database Concepts

1. **Tables:** The heart of a relational database! Tables are the "folders" holding our data.
   - **Structure:** Each table is designed with a specific structure:
     - **Columns (aka fields):** Vertical divisions. Each column defines one piece of data we store (e.g., a customer's name, product price, order date).
     - **Rows (aka records):** Horizontal entries. Each row represents a single, unique 'item' that follows the table's structure.
2. **Data Types:** Each column's data has a specific type, ensuring consistency and making SQL operations possible. Examples include:

- Text (STRING): Names, addresses, etc.
- Numbers (INTEGER, FLOAT): Whole numbers, decimals for quantities, prices, etc.
- Dates/Times (DATE, TIME): For tracking timestamps, durations, etc.
- Boolean (TRUE/FALSE): Logical values (e.g., an order being 'shipped' or not).

3. Relationships: The real magic! SQL works best when tables are designed with links:
   - Keys: These act like ID tags to identify rows and create connections:
     - Primary Key: A unique identifier for each row in a table (e.g. 'CustomerID', 'OrderID'). Every table *must* have a primary key.
     - Foreign Key: A column in one table that links to the primary key of another, establishing a relationship between the information in two tables.

Let's Visualize with an Example

Imagine an online store. Here's a simplified look at how their database might be structured using SQL logic:

- **Customer Table**
  - CustomerID (Primary Key)
  - FirstName (Text)
  - LastName (Text)
  - Email (Text)
- **Orders Table**
  - OrderID (Primary Key)
  - CustomerID (Foreign Key - links to Customer table)
  - OrderDate (Date)
  - TotalAmount (Number)
- **Product Table**
  - ProductID (Primary Key)

- ○ ProductName (Text)
- ○ Price (Number)

Why this Structure Matters

- **No Redundancy:** Customer data only needs to be stored once, saving space.
- **Integrity:** Links prevent errors; imagine an 'OrderID' with no matching 'CustomerID'!
- **Efficient Questions:** Now SQL can answer complex questions like:
  - ○ What did a specific customer order in the past six months?
  - ○ Which products are bestsellers?

Additional Resources

- **Database Design Basics:** (https://en.wikipedia.org/wiki/Database_normalization) . A bit advanced, but helpful for big-picture understanding later.
- **Entity-Relationship Diagrams (ERDs):** A visual way of designing databases - https://www.lucidchart.com/pages/er-diagram-symbols-and-meaning. This is more useful after you get hands-on with tables.

Coming up in Part 2

In the next chapter, we'll explore the building of tables and start understanding how data goes into those database "file folders." This foundation is key to mastering the powerful language of SQL!

Understanding Databases: The SQL Perspective - Part 2

Last time, we looked at databases in theory. Now it's time to see how SQL brings your imaginary database to life, including how to build tables and put data inside them.

The Magic of SQL Commands

SQL has a specific vocabulary of commands to manage databases. Here's the focus for this chapter:

- **Data Definition Language (DDL):** For creating and modifying the *structure* of the database. The core ones we'll use are:
    - **CREATE TABLE:** Sets up a new table, outlining its columns and data types.
    - **ALTER TABLE:** Modifies the structure of an existing table (adding/removing columns, etc.).
    - **DROP TABLE:** Be careful—this *deletes* an entire table, including its data!
- **Data Manipulation Language (DML):** These commands interact with the *data* inside tables. Key for now is:
    - **INSERT:** Adds new rows (records) of data to a table.

Let's Build!

We'll use our online store example from Part 1 as our template. **Important** – Syntax (spelling, etc.) of SQL commands matters! Follow along or try this in DB Browser:

```
-- Step 1: CREATE the 'Customer' Table
CREATE TABLE Customer (
    CustomerID INTEGER PRIMARY KEY,
```

```
    FirstName TEXT,
    LastName TEXT,
    Email TEXT
);
```

- **Notes:**
  - Each line specifies a column, its data type, and (optionally) constraints like 'PRIMARY KEY.'
  - The semicolon (;) is like a period at the end of a SQL 'sentence.'

The Other Tables (Try this yourself!)

```
-- Step 2: CREATE the 'Orders' Table
CREATE TABLE Orders (
    OrderID INTEGER PRIMARY KEY,
    CustomerID INTEGER,
    OrderDate DATE,
    TotalAmount NUMBER,
    FOREIGN KEY (CustomerID) REFERENCES
Customer(CustomerID)
);


-- Step 3: CREATE the 'Product' Table
CREATE TABLE Product (
    ProductID INTEGER PRIMARY KEY,
    ProductName TEXT,
    Price NUMBER
);
```

Inserting Data

Just having empty folders means no questions for SQL to answer! Let's use INSERT:

```
-- Add customers
```

```
INSERT INTO Customer (CustomerID, FirstName,
LastName, Email)
VALUES (1, 'Alice', 'Jones', 'alice@email.com'),
       (2, 'Bob', 'Smith', 'bsmith@email.org');
```

Notes:

- Table name after `INSERT INTO`.
- VALUES lists data for a new row – data must match the order of columns in the table!
- Add products, orders (connect using keys!). **Important:** Make sure `CustomerID`s and `ProductID`s you use actually exist!

Additional Resources

- **W3Schools SQL Syntax:** https://www.w3schools.com/sql/sql_ref_keywords.asp (See sections DDL & DML.)

Where This Gets Exciting

- The SELECT command, coming up next, will let us finally ask questions of the data we've put in.
- Mastering database structure is like learning the table of contents – it unlocks what you can do with SQL!

Let's move on to the heart of it all – retrieving the data you need from your database with SQL queries!

Section 2:
Retrieving and Manipulating Data

The Art of Data Retrieval with SELECT

Ready to unlock the treasure trove of information in your database? The SELECT command is your key! In the last chapter, we filled our database "file folders." Now we'll master the art of pinpointing exactly what we want to see.

The Basic Structure of a SELECT Query

```
SELECT column1, column2, ...
FROM table_name;
```

- **SELECT:** Tells the database we want to *retrieve* data.
- **column1, column2, ... :** We choose specific columns to display. To fetch every column, use the '*' (asterisk) character.
- **FROM:** Specifies which table we're interested in querying.

Let's ask a question - Example with our Online Store

Want a list of customer names:

```
SELECT FirstName, LastName
FROM Customer;
```

Results

The database returns a neatly organized table (in DB Browser, this appears in the Results tab):

FirstName	LastName
Alice	Jones
Bob	Smith

Key Points

- **SQL Doesn't Change Your Database Itself:** Remember, a query acts like a filtered window into the underlying data.
- **Case (Usually) Doesn't Matter:** SELECT and from are interchangeable with 'select' and 'FROM' - column/table names *do* need to match precisely.

The Power of the Asterisk (*)

```
SELECT * FROM Orders;
```

- The '*' is a shortcut to display *every* column within a table.
- **Good for:** Quick exploration when you know a table is small.
- **Caution:** Excessive use of '*' with massive tables can slow down queries.

Controlling the Output - DISTINCT

Let's say you want a list of all countries where your customers reside:

```
SELECT Country FROM Customer;
```

But you might have duplicates. Here's where DISTINCT comes in:

```
SELECT DISTINCT Country FROM Customer;
```

This returns a clean list *without* repetitive values.

Additional Resources

- **W3Schools SQL SELECT:**
  https://www.w3schools.com/sql/sql_select.asp
- **SQLZoo SELECT Tutorial:** https://sqlzoo.net/wiki/SELECT

Practice Time!

Using your online store example (or a practice database):

1. List the 'ProductNames' and 'Prices' from your 'Product' table.
2. Get a count of how many different products are in your Product table (hint: combine DISTINCT with another SQL word you'll find in the resources.).
3. How many customers do you have? (Again, resources will help)

Up Next: Refining Your Queries

SELECT is the foundation, but real power lies in asking *targeted* questions. In the next chapter, we'll start using the WHERE clause to pinpoint specific data and make SQL do a lot of the detective work for us!

Refining Queries with WHERE Clauses

Think of the WHERE clause as SQL's detective toolkit. It lets you go from general questions to focused investigations within your database.

How the WHERE Clause Works

It works hand-in-hand with SELECT:

```
SELECT column1, column2, ...
FROM table_name
WHERE condition1 AND/OR condition2 ...;
```

- **WHERE:** Introduces the filtering criteria.
- **Conditions:** These use comparison operators to specify rules:
    - = (Equals),
    - <> (Not equal to),
    - > (Greater than),
    - < (Less than),
    - >= (Greater than or equal to),
    - <= (Less than or equal to)

Example: Online Store Customers

Let's find customers named 'Alice':

```
SELECT FirstName, LastName, Email
FROM Customer
WHERE FirstName = 'Alice';
```

Behind the Scenes with 'WHERE'

1. Database looks at *every row* in the 'Customer' table.
2. It checks the 'FirstName' column against the condition 'FirstName = 'Alice''.
3. Only rows where this condition is TRUE are included in the output.

Combining with AND and OR

- **AND:** Multiple conditions must *all* be true for a row to be included.

Example: Customers named 'Alice' who live in the USA:

```
... WHERE FirstName = 'Alice' AND Country =
'USA';
```

- **OR:** Rows need to match *at least one* of the specified conditions.

Example: Customers named 'Alice' OR whose order total exceeds $100:

```
... WHERE FirstName = 'Alice' OR TotalAmount >
100;
```

Important Notes

- **Quotes for Text:** Text values within conditions typically need single quotes around them (e.g., 'Alice')
- **Numeric Comparisons:** No quotes needed for numbers in comparisons.

Additional Resources

- **W3Schools SQL WHERE:**
  https://www.w3schools.com/sql/sql_where.asp
- **SQLBolt Interactive Exercises:** https://sqlbolt.com/ (See lessons focused on WHERE)

Challenges (Try these in DB Browser)

1. List products priced between 5 and 15 inclusive.
2. Find orders placed between January 1, 2023 and January 31, 2023. (**Hint:** You'll likely need the concepts of AND plus date comparisons).
3. Show how many orders *each* customer has placed (**Hint:** This will sneakily introduce a skill from our upcoming 'Advanced Query Techniques' chapter!).

The WHERE Clause Advantage

- **Efficiency:** Saves your database from sifting through unnecessary data, making queries much faster.
- **Precision:** Helps you zero in on insights hiding within the bigger picture.

Coming Up

Now that you know how to target specific data with WHERE, the next chapter focuses on advanced filtering, allowing you to ask sophisticated questions and unlock the true power of your data.

Advanced Query Techniques: Enhancing Criteria and Limiting Responses - Part 1

You've already tamed the fundamentals of SELECT and WHERE! Now, we move to the next level in controlling and analyzing your data with precision. Think of this chapter as introducing some more tools into that handy SQL detective toolkit.

Filtering Techniques

- **LIKE: For Pattern Matching**
  Often, you don't know the *exact* value you're searching for. LIKE offers wildcard characters:
    - **%: ** Matches zero, one, or many characters. Example: `FirstName LIKE 'Al%'` finds 'Alice', 'Alex', etc.
    - _ **(underscore):** Matches a *single* character. Example: `Product Name LIKE '_ouse'` finds 'Mouse', 'House', etc.

Example: Find all products containing the word 'wireless':

```
SELECT * FROM Product
WHERE ProductName LIKE '%wireless%';
```

- **IN: Checking Against a List**

Instead of multiple OR conditions, IN offers a shortcut:

Example: Show customers from Canada, Germany, or the USA:

```
SELECT * FROM Customer
```

```
WHERE Country IN ('Canada', 'Germany', 'USA');
```

- **BETWEEN: Focusing on Ranges**

Handy for numbers and dates:

Example: Find orders placed between October 1st and October 15th, 2023:

```
SELECT * FROM Orders
WHERE OrderDate BETWEEN '2023-10-01' AND
'2023-10-15';
```

Limiting Results: TOP, LIMIT, and OFFSET

Real-world datasets can be massive. Sometimes you just need a "quick sample".

- **TOP (SQL Server):** Example: Only see the top five highest order totals:

```
SELECT TOP 5 OrderID, TotalAmount
FROM Orders;
```

- **LIMIT (MySQL, SQLite, PostgreSQL):** Same purpose, slightly different syntax:

```
SELECT OrderID, TotalAmount
FROM Orders
LIMIT 5;
```

- **OFFSET:** Skipping a set number of rows. Often used *with* LIMIT/TOP for paging through large results:

```
... LIMIT 10 OFFSET 5;
```

` ` `   (Shows rows 6-15).

Important: Each database system (MySQL, SQL Server, etc.) may have minor syntax differences for these concepts.

Additional Resources

- **W3Schools SQL LIKE :**
  https://www.w3schools.com/sql/sql_like.asp
- **W3Schools SQL IN:**
  https://www.w3schools.com/sql/sql_in.asp
- **W3Schools SQL BETWEEN:**
  https://www.w3schools.com/sql/sql_between.asp

Practice

1. Find all products whose names end with 'pad'.
2. Display orders with 'Shipped' status or 'Processing' status.
3. Using only your 'Customer' table, get a list of the top 10 cities with the most customers. (**Hint:** This will stretch your thinking – try it! We'll cover a full solution in Part 2).

Up Next: Even More Refining & Combining

Part 2 dives into subqueries (queries within queries!), powerful sorting techniques, and the beginnings of calculating directly within SQL! These skills, along with what you've learned here, unlock even more valuable insights from your data.

Advanced Query Techniques: Enhancing Criteria and Limiting Responses - Part 2

Last chapter we dipped our toes into more powerful filtering and control. Now let's take the plunge and see how SQL enables even more complex questions about our data.

The Power of ORDER BY

Often you don't want results in 'whatever' order the database feels like giving. ORDER BY lets you sort things neatly:

```
SELECT *
FROM Product
ORDER BY Price; -- Default is ascending (low to high)
```

- **ASC vs. DESC:**
    - ASC (ascending) is the default if you don't specify.
    - DESC (descending) for reverse order (high to low).

- **Multiple Levels:** Example: Sort products by category, then alphabetically within each category:

```
... ORDER BY Category ASC, ProductName ASC;
```

Calculating within SQL

Databases go beyond storage - let's do some math!

- **COUNT():** Get the *number* of rows matching your criteria:

```
SELECT COUNT(*)
FROM Orders
WHERE OrderDate >= '2023-12-01';   -- Orders in
December 2023
```

- **SUM():** Totals up a numeric column:

```
SELECT SUM(TotalAmount) AS TotalSales
FROM Orders;
```

- **AVG():** Find averages. Example: Average order value? Use SUM() and COUNT() together!

Important: Using calculations often involves giving the resulting output a nickname ("AS TotalSales" in the example)

Subqueries: Queries within Queries

Imagine nesting dolls – a subquery is a SELECT inside another. Its result is used by the outer query:

Example: How much above-average was our most expensive order?

```
SELECT MAX(TotalAmount) - (SELECT
AVG(TotalAmount) FROM Orders) AS
DifferenceAboveAvg
FROM Orders;
```

- **Inner Workings:**
    1. Inner SELECT AVG(TotalAmount) FROM Orders runs first, producing the average order value.
    2. Outer query subtracts this average from the highest order total ('MAX(TotalAmount)').

Additional Resources

- **W3Schools SQL ORDER BY:**
  https://www.w3schools.com/sql/sql_orderby.asp
- **SQL Tutorial ORDER BY and Calculations:**
  https://www.sqltutorial.org/ (Search within their site)

Challenges

1. List your top 5 customers based on the *number* of orders they've placed (not total amount).
2. What's the difference in price between your most expensive and least expensive product?
3. Can you solve the "top 10 cities with the most customers" challenge from Part 1? (**Don't worry, there's a whole upcoming chapter on aggregating data later!)

Just the Beginning

We're venturing deeper! Combining calculations, subqueries, and advanced filtering unlocks analysis you couldn't easily do by exporting your data elsewhere.

Prepare for ORDER BY

In the next chapter, we'll continue expanding our control over how results are displayed with ORDER BY, focusing on ordering results in groups and more precise output customization.

Structuring Data Output: The Power of ORDER BY – Part 1

You already know the basics of ORDER BY to sort results. But ORDER BY unlocks much more than simple alphabetizing! Let's delve into controlling the way you *view* your data, adding clarity and focusing on the insights that matter.

Ordering by Multiple Columns

Real-world scenarios rarely involve simple one-column sorting. Remember: SQL processes ORDER BY from left to right in your query.

Example: Online Store, sorting products:

```
SELECT ProductName, Category, Price
FROM Product
ORDER BY Category ASC, Price DESC;
```

Results:

- **First:** Products are grouped by 'Category' in ascending order (e.g., Apparel, Electronics, Home Goods).
- **Then, Within Each Category:** Products are sorted by 'Price' in descending order (highest to lowest).

Controlling Null Values

- **NULL:** Represents missing or unknown data (empty cells in our spreadsheets).
- **Default Behavior:** SQL typically puts NULL values at the end of the order.
- **Controlling Nulls:** If you prefer, use the following:

- ○ **NULLS FIRST** Places NULL values *before* non-null values
- ○ **NULLS LAST** Places NULL values *after* non-null values

Example: Show customers, but place those missing an email at the top to remind you to follow up:

```
SELECT FirstName, LastName, Email
FROM Customer
ORDER BY Email NULLS FIRST;
```

Beyond Numbers and Text: Date and Time

ORDER BY works seamlessly with DATE and TIME data types. Let's find those recent orders:

```
SELECT OrderID, CustomerID, OrderDate
FROM Orders
ORDER BY OrderDate DESC;   -- Newest orders on top
```

Ordering with Calculations

Remember those calculations we introduced in the last chapter? You can order by them, too! Say you want to see product price *including* a hypothetical 10% discount:

```
SELECT ProductName, Price, (Price * 0.9) AS
DiscountedPrice
FROM Product
ORDER BY DiscountedPrice ASC;
```

Additional Resources

- **W3Schools on NULL Handling:**
  https://www.w3schools.com/sql/sql_null_values.asp

- **Ordering by Date/Time:** Different databases may have subtle differences (date formatting, etc.). Search for '[database name] order by date' (example: 'MySQL order by date')

Practice

1. Display products, ordered first by whether they're in stock or not ('InStock' – assume this is a True/False column), then alphabetically by ProductName.
2. List orders, but group them first by whether they've shipped ('ShippedDate' will be null if not yet shipped). Within each group, show the latest order dates first.

Get Comfortable with 'How' You See Data

Sometimes, the *order* in which you view results is crucial for revealing meaningful information. Mastering ORDER BY means SQL isn't just retrieving data – it's presenting it in a way that empowers your analysis.

Part 2 – Going Further

In the next chapter, we'll go deeper with ORDER BY, including the concept of 'partitions' for even more fine-grained sorting and customization for the most insightful results.

Structuring Data Output: The Power of ORDER BY – Part 2

In Part 1, we focused on sorting our overall results. Now let's dive into more structured ordering within *groups* or sets of data using some advanced, yet incredibly useful, ORDER BY techniques.

Ordering within Groups – Introducing Partitions

Imagine you need sales totals *per month* for the past year. You want each month's orders organized from the highest to the lowest sale.

We achieve this with PARTITION BY:

```
SELECT
  MONTH(OrderDate) AS OrderMonth,
  SUM(TotalAmount) AS MonthlySales
FROM Orders
WHERE OrderDate >= '2023-01-01' -- Only for year
2023
GROUP BY MONTH(OrderDate) -- We'll explain GROUP
BY in a future chapter
ORDER BY OrderMonth, MonthlySales DESC;
```

- **How It Works:**
    1. PARTITION BY MONTH(OrderDate) tells SQL to think in terms of separate 'buckets' per month.
    2. *Within each month* (OrderMonth), the ORDER BY MonthlySales DESC sorts individual order totals from highest to lowest.

Window Functions: Analysis superpowers

These provide calculations across sets of rows – perfect for analysis without changing the base data:

- **ROW_NUMBER():** Assigns a sequential number to each row *within a partition* (or your overall result if no partition exists).

Example: Ranking each customer's orders by expense (most expensive = 1):

```
SELECT
  CustomerID, OrderID, TotalAmount,
  ROW_NUMBER() OVER (PARTITION BY CustomerID
ORDER BY TotalAmount DESC) AS OrderRank
FROM Orders;
```

Additional Resources

- **SQLBolt Partition By Tutorial:** https://docs.microsoft.com/en-us/sql/t-sql/queries/select-over-clause-transact-sql?view=sql-server-ver15
- **Window Functions Guide:** Database-specific, as syntax might vary slightly. Search for '[Database Name] window functions'

Practice Exercises

1. Modify the sales report query to include a column showing *how many* orders contributed to each 'MonthlySales' total. (**Hint:** COUNT() function might be useful)
2. Imagine you're building a leaderboard. Display customers with a rank based on their total spending across *all* their orders.

Why This Matters

These methods let you answer sophisticated questions without complex changes to your database structure:

- **Trends Within Groups:** Did our top-selling product category change month to month?
- **Ranking:** Who were our most frequent shoppers, not just big spenders?
- **Focused Analysis:** Which product in *each category* performed worst (for targeted discounts, etc.)?

A Note on Complexity

We're approaching an area where SQL intersects with broader statistical analysis. Don't worry about mastering this all at once! It's about awareness of what tools exist.

Coming up: JOINs - The Heart of Relational Data

So far, we've analyzed data largely from single tables. But the true power of *relational* databases lies in connections. Soon, we'll start using JOIN to combine information across multiple tables in exciting ways!

Exploring JOIN Operations: The Basics

So far, we've asked questions within single tables. But remember, the magic of relational databases lies in connections between those tables. That's where JOIN enters the picture! Think of JOIN like a bridge-builder for your data.

Why JOIN Matters

Real-world questions rarely live neatly within one table. Example: We want a list of customer names *and* their corresponding order totals.

- Problem: Customer names are in the Customer table. Order totals are in the Orders table.
- Solution: A JOIN lets us bring these together based on a shared relationship.

Our Tool: The INNER JOIN

The most common is the INNER JOIN. Here's how it works:

```
SELECT FirstName, LastName, OrderID, TotalAmount
FROM Customer
INNER JOIN Orders ON Customer.CustomerID =
Orders.CustomerID;
```

Let's break it down:

- **SELECT:** As always, indicates columns we want to see.
- **FROM and INNER JOIN:** Tells SQL which tables to link.
- **ON:** The *crux* of it all! Specifies how tables relate:

- ○ Customer.CustomerID = Orders.CustomerID – Our bridge! Only rows where this condition is true will be included in the result.

Visualizing the INNER JOIN

Imagine overlapping your 'Customer' and 'Orders' tables, aligning rows where those 'CustomerID' values match. INNER JOIN gives you this combined view.

Behind the Scenes

1. Database looks at the first row in 'Customer'.
2. It searches 'Orders' for rows with the matching 'CustomerID'.
3. When a match is found, data from *both* rows is combined into a single row in your output!
4. Process repeats for every row in 'Customer'.

Important Notes

- **Matching Columns = The Key:** The data type of the columns you join ON must match (both numbers, both text, etc.).
- **Aliases - Nicknames for Tables:** In bigger queries, it's common to give tables shorter names:

```
... FROM Customer AS c
    INNER JOIN Orders AS o
    ON c.CustomerID = o.CustomerID;
```

Additional Resources

- **W3Schools SQL JOIN Types:** https://www.w3schools.com/sql/sql_join.asp – Focus on INNER JOIN.

Practice: Get Hands-On

1. Write a query to show Product names from your 'Product' table *and* their associated category (assuming you have a 'Category' table and related columns).
2. Get ambitious! List customer names, their city, and the total number of orders they've placed.

The Doorway to Powerful Analysis

JOIN opens up a world of questions you couldn't answer before:

- Which products are most popular among customers in a specific country?
- Have some customers never placed an order?
- Do certain product categories sell better in specific months?

Coming Up

We've only scratched the surface! Next, we'll cover other JOIN types for even more versatile ways to explore the rich connections within your relational data.

Exploring JOIN Operations: Intermediate Concepts

In the last chapter, we unlocked the world of INNER JOIN. Now, let's add more versatility to the way we connect our data with additional join types and learn to combine a table with *itself*!

Beyond INNER JOIN

- **LEFT (OUTER) JOIN:** Think "All from the Left".
  - Includes *all* rows from the table on the left side of the JOIN keyword, even if no match exists on the right.
  - Use Case: Finding customers who have *never* placed an order (they'd exist in 'Customer' but not 'Orders').

```
SELECT FirstName, LastName, OrderID --  OrderID
will be NULL for unmatched customers
FROM Customer AS c
LEFT JOIN Orders AS o ON c.CustomerID =
o.CustomerID;
```

- **RIGHT (OUTER) JOIN:** The 'mirror image' of LEFT JOIN.
  - Includes *all* rows from the table on the right side of the JOIN, even if no match on the left.
  - Use Case: Rare, but let's say you temporarily added some products to a 'NewProducts' table without assigning them to an order. A RIGHT JOIN could ensure they aren't left out of reports.

Important: Most databases support both a LEFT and RIGHT version. Focus on one to master the concept, then learning its sister type is easy!

JOINs are Flexible

You can combine all learned join types with WHERE, ORDER BY, and the whole range of SQL techniques – they are not one or the other! It's about getting the right outcome!

Joining a Table to Itself? (Self-Joins)

What if we want to compare data *within* a table? This is common with hierarchical structures:

Example: An 'Employee' table where the 'ManagerID' column links to an 'EmployeeID' of that employee's manager. Here's how to see employees *and* their manager's name:

```
SELECT e1.FirstName AS Employee, e2.FirstName AS
Manager
FROM Employee AS e1
INNER JOIN Employee AS e2 ON e1.ManagerID =
e2.EmployeeID;
```

- **Note:** Aliases ('e1', 'e2') are *essential* here! Otherwise, SQL wouldn't know which 'FirstName' you want!

Practice Time

1. Modify the 'customers with no orders' query to show *only* customers without an order, cleaning up those NULL values.
2. Imagine a table storing messages like a mini-forum:
    - MessageID, ParentMessageID (null if a top-level post), Content, Timestamp Write a query using a self-join to display both original posts *and* their immediate replies side-by-side.

Caution: Going Too Far

It's *possible* to chain many joins (table A → table B → table C…).
BUT:

- Performance impact: The more joins, the harder your database works. Think carefully if it's necessary.
- Readability: Complex multi-joins make queries hard to understand, maintain, and modify.

Strategy First, Tools Second

Always begin a complex analysis by sketching out the relationship between information first. Don't jump to code! Then, figure out which join tools bring that mental model to life in your query.

Next Up: Even More JOIN Power

There may be situations where JOINs combined with techniques like subqueries will provide optimal results. As your SQL fluency grows, you'll learn to combine tools strategically!

Exploring JOIN Operations: Advanced Strategies

You now have a powerful set of JOIN tools at your disposal! Let's look at some less common scenarios where joins flex their muscle and ways to use SQL's other features for similar outcomes.

Joining on Multiple Conditions

Sometimes the link between tables isn't so simple. The ON condition within your join can handle this:

Example: We track product returns in a 'Returns' table:

- OrderID
- ProductID
- ReturnDate

To see returned products *AND* the original order date:

```
SELECT ProductName, Orders.OrderID, OrderDate,
ReturnDate
FROM Returns
INNER JOIN Orders ON Returns.OrderID =
Orders.OrderID
INNER JOIN Product ON Returns.ProductID =
Product.ProductID;
```

Joining More Than Two Tables

There's no theoretical limit to chaining joins! But use with caution as queries become harder to read and may cause slowdowns.

Think strategically: Is it *necessary*? Would it be better to break down complex questions into smaller queries?

Outer Joins vs. Subqueries (Sometimes!)

Let's revisit the "customers with no orders" problem. Here's an alternative to a LEFT JOIN:

```
SELECT FirstName, LastName
FROM Customer
WHERE CustomerID NOT IN (SELECT DISTINCT
CustomerID FROM Orders);
```

- **How It Works:**
    - The subquery gets distinct 'CustomerID' values which *do* exist in 'Orders'. *
    - The WHERE clause excludes customers whose IDs appear in those results.

Performance Note: Which is *faster* depends on your database, how your data is indexed, etc. **Experiment** with large datasets!

Beyond Joins: 'Correlated Subqueries'

These go deeper! A correlated subquery is a subquery with a condition referencing the *outer* query. Example: Finding products where **no** order quantity exceeds 10:

```
SELECT ProductName
FROM Product AS p
WHERE NOT EXISTS (
    SELECT 1 FROM Orders o
    WHERE o.ProductID = p.ProductID AND Quantity >
10
);
```

- **Key Idea:** The inner subquery runs repeatedly **for each row** in the 'Product' table.

Challenges

1. Imagine an 'Invoice' table (InvoiceID, CustomerID, InvoiceDate) and 'Invoice_LineItems' table (InvoiceLineID, InvoiceID, ProductID, Quantity, LineItemPrice). Write a query showing: Customers, Total Invoiced Amount per Customer, the Number of Invoices. **(Hint:** You'll need joins plus some of the calculation concepts from earlier chapters).
2. Can you rewrite the above challenge to solve it *without* JOINs at all, only subqueries?

A Word of Caution

Complex joins/subqueries can be powerful. But if you find yourself writing SQL that's impossible to understand a week later... there might be a better way!

- **Readability:** Comment your complex queries to explain your logic – your future self will thank you!
- **Alternatives:** Can the database structure be improved? Would storing a calculated "total invoices per customer" (and updating when orders change) simplify things?

The Big Picture

SQL gives you options! The 'best' solution is about balance: clarity, performance, and fitting the way your specific database works under the hood. This mastery comes with experience!

Synthesizing Data: Techniques for Combining Results

Until now, we've focused on getting precise *rows* of data from our tables. But often, we want summarized information: counts, averages, trends hidden *within* our detail data. That's where the power of aggregation comes in!

The Key Pillar: GROUP BY

Usually works hand-in-hand with the following aggregate functions:

- **COUNT():** Total rows in a group
- **SUM():** Adds up values in a group
- **AVG():** Calculates the average within a group
- **MIN():** Finds the smallest value in a group
- **MAX():** Finds the largest value in a group

Example: Sales per Product Category:

```
SELECT Category, SUM(TotalAmount) AS TotalSales
FROM Orders
INNER JOIN Product ON Orders.ProductID =
Product.ProductID
GROUP BY Category;
```

- **How it works:**
    1. GROUP BY Category tells SQL to treat rows with the same 'Category' as a single unit.
    2. SUM(TotalAmount) is calculated *for each category group*.

Important Notes:

- Columns in your SELECT must either be included in GROUP BY or have an aggregate function applied.
- WHERE is still your friend! Apply filters *before* grouping if needed.

HAVING: Filtering Groups (Like WHERE, but After)

Let's say you only want categories with total sales exceeding $1000:

```
... (Same query as above)
HAVING SUM(TotalAmount) > 1000;
```

- HAVING acts like WHERE but operates on the summarized groups created by GROUP BY.

Calculating Alongside Detail

What if we want sales per category *and* individual order totals? You can mix grouped and ungrouped columns!

```
SELECT Category, OrderID, TotalAmount,
SUM(TotalAmount) OVER () AS GrandTotalSales
FROM Orders
INNER JOIN Product ON Orders.ProductID =
Product.ProductID;
```

- We added the OVER() clause - this calculates our SUM() across ALL data, repeating the result on each row for comparison.

Additional Resources

- **W3Schools SQL Aggregate Functions:** https://www.w3schools.com/sql/sql_groupby.asp

Practice

1. Get the number of customers from each country.
2. Find the average order value per month for the past year.
3. List each product, the most recent date it was ordered, and the total quantity sold across all orders.

Beyond Basic Reporting

These tools unlock analysis unavailable with raw data:

- **Spotting Trends:** Monthly 'SUM(TotalAmount)' helps answer, "Are sales growing?"
- **Outliers:** 'MIN()' and 'MAX()' within groups can highlight unusually expensive orders, etc.
- **Proportions:** Calculate a category's percentage of total sales by combining a SUM() at the category level with an OVER() to get the grand total.

Key Takeaways

- **Master the Mechanics:** Practice building these queries, so they become intuitive.
- **Think Analytically:** Before writing code, ask: "What pattern or insight am I trying to reveal from my detailed data?"

Section 3:
SQL Data Types, Mathematical Operations, and Functions

SQL Data Types and Mathematical Foundations

Beyond telling databases *how* to store data, data types are essential for SQL to function correctly. Think of them as building blocks, and you must select the right type for the job! They also underpin any calculations we want our queries to perform.

Common Data Types and Their Importance

1. **Numeric Types**
    - **Integers:** (Ex: … -2, -1, 0, 1, 2…) Whole numbers only. Used for quantities, IDs, etc.
        - **Important:** Different databases offer types like 'SMALLINT', 'BIGINT' – each has a maximum storable size. Choose wisely for efficiency!
    - **Floating-Point:** (Ex: 3.14, -25.8) Handle decimals. For prices, measurements, anything requiring accuracy with fractions.
        - **Caution:** Floating-point math can have tiny rounding errors – critical for financial systems? Specialized 'fixed decimal' types are a must.
2. **Text Types**

- VARCHAR / CHAR: "Variable character" / "Character". Flexible storage for names, addresses, and other text.
  - **Key Difference:** CHAR is fixed size (padded with spaces); VARCHAR is more space-efficient but slightly slower in some cases.

3. **Date and Time**
   - **DATE:** Stores year, month, day.
   - **TIME:** Stores hour, minute, second.
   - **TIMESTAMP / DATETIME:** Combines both. Great for order timestamps, event logs, etc.
     - **Watch Out:** Storing timezone info along with dates gets complex! May involve advanced types in your specific database.

4. **Boolean**
   - **TRUE / FALSE:** Perfect for flags (Product 'InStock', Email 'IsSubscribed'), logical columns used in query filtering.

Why Do Data Types Matter?

- **Sorting & Comparisons:** Mixing numbers and text in one column? Your ORDER BY will do strange things!
- **Mathematical Accuracy:** Prices stored as text won't add up or subtract reliably.
- **Storage Optimization:** Giant text blocks for a simple 'Status' field waste database space.
- **Data Protection:** Well-chosen types help prevent incorrect input into your tables.

Database Variations

Every database (SQLite, MySQL, etc.) has subtle naming differences for types. Always reference the documentation of your specific system!

Mathematical Foundations

- **Order of Operations:** SQL follows these (think back to school: Parentheses, Exponents, Multiply/Divide, Add/Subtract). Crucial when writing formulas within queries.
- **NULL is NOT Zero!**
  - NULL = unknown/missing. AVG( ) on a column with a NULL ignores that row. Handling empty cells requires logic (covered later with functions).

Practice

1. Look at your sample database. For each column in your tables, note its current data type. Think: Is it the most appropriate choice? Could anything be improved?
2. **Challenge:** Find a SQL function online that lets you extract *just the month* from a date column. Then try to select records from a hypothetical table containing a 'HireDate' column, filtering using that function to show only people hired on February. **Don't worry yet if you struggle – we'll tackle functions soon!**

Think Like an Architect

Choosing the right data types is foundational, making your SQL work both reliably and efficiently. Well-structured data helps your queries fly!

Next Up

Now, let's see how SQL applies mathematical knowledge, giving you real analytical power and the ability to handle different data types within your queries.

SQL Data Types and Mathematical Applications

Last chapter, we laid the groundwork. Now let's see data types in action! SQL not only stores your data but provides tools to operate *on* data types, revealing even more insights hidden within your stored information.

Basic Arithmetic

You've already seen this with COUNT( ), SUM( ), and AVG( ). We can perform other mathematical operations right within our SELECT clause:

```
SELECT
    ProductID,
    Price,
    Quantity,
    (Price * Quantity) AS LineTotal,
    Price * 1.08 AS PriceWithTax -- Assuming  8%
tax
FROM Order_LineItems;
```

- **Note:** Operators follow standard order of operations! Use parentheses to enforce specific order if needed.

Type Conversion: Sometimes Necessary

Databases can get grumpy about mixing types incorrectly:

- **Implicit Conversion:** Often handled for you under-the-hood. Example: Database might turn a number "60" into the text "60" to fit into a text-based calculation. Best to not rely on this if possible!

- **Explicit Conversion:** Use special functions for clarity, avoiding surprises, especially when data comes from varying sources:
  Example:

```
SELECT ProductID, YEAR(CAST(OrderDate AS DATE))
AS OrderYear
FROM Orders;
```

  - ○ We assume your 'OrderDate' is a datetime type. CAST() takes that value temporarily treats it as 'DATE' allowing the YEAR() function to extract the year component correctly.

Date & Time Math

- **Differences:** Calculating days between orders:

```
 SELECT OrderID, OrderDate, ShippedDate,
        DATEDIFF(day, OrderDate, ShippedDate) AS
ShippingDays
 FROM Orders;
```

- **Adding/Subtracting Intervals:** Find orders due to ship soon:

```
SELECT OrderID, OrderDate,
      DATE_ADD(OrderDate, INTERVAL 7 DAY) AS
DueDate
FROM Orders WHERE ShippedDate IS NULL;
```

Caution: Date functions are where databases vary most! Refer to documentation for the correct syntax in *your* database (search: '[Database Type] date functions').

Beyond Retrieval: Calculations Change Data

While this chapter has focused on calculating values for display via SELECT, these same math techniques are employed during database update processes, letting you adjust stored values directly

Practice

1. If there's a 10% discount on any product costing over $50, write a query to display ProductName, standard Price, and the Price after the potential discount.
2. Imagine a subscription table: 'StartDate', 'LengthInMonths'. Get a list of still-active users by calculating an 'EndDate', then filter to where that calculated 'EndDate' is in the future.

The Importance of Correct Typing

Math may seem like a side topic, but getting precise and meaningful results within SQL *depends* on the data type foundation you laid earlier. Mismatches cause trouble!

The Versatility of Compound Select Queries

So far, we've used SELECT to fetch columns "as is" from our tables. However, SQL enables on-the-fly calculations and logic directly within this clause, creating dynamic output not found as stored data within your database.

Case When: Conditional Logic (Decoding Values)

Imagine a status code: 'P' = Pending, 'S' = Shipped, 'C' = Cancelled. For readability, a report should display the full words. Here's CASE WHEN:

```
SELECT OrderID,
       CASE
           WHEN OrderStatus = 'P' THEN 'Pending'
           WHEN OrderStatus = 'S' THEN 'Shipped'
           WHEN OrderStatus = 'C' THEN
'Cancelled'
           ELSE 'Unknown Status'  -- Handle
unexpected
       END AS StatusDescription
FROM Orders;
```

- **How it Works:**
  - Each WHEN is a condition, followed by THEN and the value to output *if that condition is true*
  - ELSE (optional) is your catch-all default.

IFNULL - Tidying Up NULL Values

Missing data? Replace those uninformative 'NULL' displays:

```
SELECT FirstName, LastName,
```

```
    IFNULL(Email, 'No Email Provided') AS Email
FROM Customer;
```

- IFNULL takes two arguments: the column/expression, and the desired value if the original is NULL.

Concatenation: Combining Text

Join strings within your output. Syntax varies slightly per database:

```
-- Common in MySQL/SQLite:
SELECT CONCAT(FirstName, ' ', LastName) AS
FullName FROM Customer;


--  SQL Server / PostgreSQL often use + :
SELECT FirstName + ' ' + LastName AS FullName
FROM Customer;
```

Beyond Simple Formulas

Nearly any calculation from the last chapter can be embedded within your SELECT:

```
SELECT ...,
        UnitPrice * (1 - DiscountPercent) AS
FinalPrice,
        ...
```

Additional Resources:

- **'String Functions in SQL':**
  https://www.w3schools.com/sql/sql_ref_string_functions.asp

Practice

1. You have a small 'ProductTypes' table: 'TypeID', 'TypeName'. Enhance your Product display to include not

just 'Product Name' but "Product Name (Category Name)".
(**Hint:** Join + logic).

2. Simulate a 3-tier rating system. If 'TotalAmount' of an order
   is:
   ○ < $50: Assign it "Bronze" status
   ○ 50-150: "Silver" status
   ○ Anything higher: "Gold" status

The Power of Dynamic Output

1. **User Friendly Applications:** Your database might store
   codes, but your app can use SQL to decode them during
   display, improving user experience.
2. **Ad-Hoc Analysis:** Don't need to modify the database
   schema – calculate and transform data on demand while
   doing exploratory analysis.
3. **Derived Columns:** Sometimes, calculations/combinations
   exist across *multiple* rows... this is hinting at future skills
   (subqueries!) where such values become usable as if they
   were their own separate column!

Note on Complexity: Overly complex SELECT clauses can impact
query speed. Sometimes it's more appropriate to store
pre-calculated data IF a column is always used this way and
needs the best possible performance.

Next: Modifying & Transforming Existing Data

We've unleashed the ability to reshape data as it's *retrieved*. Soon,
we'll learn how SQL allows you to alter, transform, and clean the
data within the tables themselves.

Data Transformation Techniques

In the complex landscape of data, raw values often need adjustments or refinements to make them suitable for our specific analysis purposes. This chapter delves into several essential SQL techniques used to transform data effectively within your database.

Key Transformation Scenarios

Before diving into techniques, let's outline common reasons you might perform data transformations:

- **Cleaning and Standardization:** Correcting typos, enforcing consistent capitalization, unifying date formats, or handling missing values.
- **Reshaping:** Changing the structure of data, such as pivoting rows into columns or vice versa.
- **Calculations:** Performing arithmetic operations, creating derived values, or generating complex aggregations.
- **Categorization:** Converting continuous data into categories (e.g., age brackets), assigning labels, or bucketing values.

Common Techniques

1. **String Manipulation Functions**
   - **CONCAT():** Combines multiple strings.
     - Example: CONCAT(first_name, ' ', last_name)
   - **SUBSTRING():** Extracts a portion of a string.
     - Example: SUBSTRING(address, 1, 10) (First 10 characters of an address)
   - **LOWER(), UPPER():** Convert a string to lower or uppercase, respectively.

- TRIM(): Removes leading and trailing whitespace.

2. **Date and Time Functions**
   - **EXTRACT():** Retrieves specific components (year, month, day, etc.) from dates.
     - Example: EXTRACT(YEAR FROM order_date)
   - **DATE_ADD(), DATE_SUB():** Add or subtract intervals from dates.
   - **DATE_FORMAT():** Format dates and times into various representations.

3. **Conditional Logic with CASE Statements**
   - Create new columns or transform existing ones based on multiple conditions.

Example:
```
CASE
  WHEN sales > 1000 THEN 'High Sales'
  WHEN sales BETWEEN 500 AND 1000 THEN 'Medium
Sales'
  ELSE 'Low Sales'
END AS sales_category
```

   -

4. **Numeric Calculations**
   - Use arithmetic operators (+, -, *, /), modulo (%), and functions like ROUND(), ABS(), CEIL(), FLOOR().

5. **Type Conversion Functions**
   - **CAST():** Explicitly converts a value from one data type to another.
     - Example: CAST(order_id AS VARCHAR(10))
   - **TO_CHAR(), TO_NUMBER():** Similar to CAST, with some dialect-specific variations.

Additional Resources

The specific functions available may vary slightly depending on the SQL dialect you're using. Here are resources to deepen your knowledge:

- **W3Schools SQL Functions:**
  https://www.w3schools.com/sql/sql_ref_functions.asp
- **SQL Server Functions (many apply broadly):**
  https://learn.microsoft.com/en-us/sql/t-sql/functions/functions
- **PostgreSQL Functions (if applicable):**
  https://www.postgresql.org/docs/current/functions.html

Practice Makes Perfect

Data transformation is a hands-on skill. Utilize DB Browser to experiment with these techniques on sample datasets or your own project data.

Data Transformation Strategies

The previous chapters provided you with powerful SQL tools for individual data manipulations. Now, it's time to step back and think strategically about the process of data transformation as a whole. A well-planned strategy ensures clean, meaningful, and analysis-ready data.

Understanding Your Goals

Before you touch a single line of SQL, answer these core questions:

- **What are you trying to achieve?** What analyses do you intend, or what are your reporting needs? Data should be shaped to answer specific business questions.
- **What is the quality of your source data?** Are there errors, inconsistencies, or missing values? Cleaning and preprocessing is often a major step.
- **What format is best for your end purpose?** Consider how the transformed data will be used (visualization tools, machine learning models, etc.).

Key Strategic Phases

1. **Data Profiling and Assessment:**
   - **Inspect Data Types:** Ensure columns are correctly classified (numeric, text, dates, etc.).
   - **Statistical Exploration:** Use summaries like COUNT, MIN, MAX, and AVERAGE to reveal ranges, anomalies, and potential issues.
   - **Null Value Analysis:** Identify the extent and patterns of missing data.
2. **Data Cleaning:**

- Outlier Handling: Decide how to address extreme or implausible values (remove, transform, or set them to null).
- Data Standardization: Enforce consistent formatting (e.g., date formats, currency representation, address abbreviations).
- Error Correction: Address misspellings, inconsistencies, or incorrect entries, potentially employing external reference data.

3. **Data Transformation (Core Techniques):**
   - Normalization/Denormalization: Consider appropriate database design principles based on the complexity of your queries and required performance.
   - Aggregation: Use SQL's summarizing functions (SUM, AVG, COUNT) to create new views on your data.
   - Feature Creation: Derive new data features that could lead to insights within your analysis. For example, calculating 'days since last purchase' from an order date.

4. **Data Validation:**
   - Logic Checks: Implement rules using SQL logic to verify data integrity after transformations.
   - Cross-Referencing: If multiple sources were used, verify consistency across them.

Best Practices

- **Documentation:** Keep track of the specific transformations and cleaning applied to your data.
- **Iteration:** Data transformation is rarely a linear process. You may cycle back to cleaning or refinement steps as you analyze.

- **Automation:** When you have predictable or repeated transformation needs, consider scripts or ETL tools for efficiency.

Case Study Example

Imagine a dataset of product sales.

- **Profiling:** Reveals an inconsistent 'Price' column (some items have currency symbols, others don't).
- **Cleaning:** Standardizes prices to numeric format, addresses missing values (maybe set to average for that product category).
- **Transformation:** Adds new columns:
  - 'profit_margin' calculated from price and known cost information
  - 'sales_category' by binning price into 'high', 'medium', 'low'
- **Validation:** Check that profit margin calculation is correct, verify no negative values are introduced.

Inserting and Modifying Data: Essentials

So far, you've mastered retrieving and transforming data to uncover information. Now, it's time to learn how to directly change the content of your databases. SQL provides core commands for adding, updating, and even deleting data in a controlled manner.

Fundamentals of Insertion

- **The INSERT INTO Statement:**

```
INSERT INTO table_name (column1, column2, ...)
VALUES (value1, value2, ...);
```

  - ○ **Important:** The order of values *must* match the order of the columns. Data types must be compatible (e.g., text values in quotes).
- **Inserting Partial Data:** Explicitly listing columns lets you insert values into a subset of a table's columns. Other columns, if they allow nulls or have defaults, will take these values.
- **Inserting from Another Table:** Using a SELECT subquery:

```
INSERT INTO destination_table (column1, column2,
...)
SELECT column1, column2, ...
FROM source_table
WHERE ...; -- Optional criteria to filter source
data
```

Updating Existing Data

- **The UPDATE Statement:**

```
UPDATE table_name
SET column1 = new_value1, column2 = new_value2,
...
WHERE condition; -- **Crucial** to avoid updating
all rows!
```

- **Conditional Updates:** Utilize the WHERE clause to target specific rows for modification. Forgetting the WHERE clause may update all records in the table!
- **Updating with Calculations:**

```
UPDATE products
SET price = price * 1.10; -- Increase prices by
10%
```

Deleting Records

- **The DELETE Statement:**

```
DELETE FROM table_name
WHERE condition; -- Omitting the WHERE clause is
dangerous!
```

  ○ **Extreme Caution:** DELETE operations in most cases permanently remove data. Consider backups or "soft-delete" strategies if appropriate.

Key Practices and Considerations

- **Understanding Datatypes:** Ensure the values you insert or update align with the column's defined data type. Mismatches can cause errors or unexpected results.
- **Constraints and Rules:** Your database may have rules (e.g., unique keys, foreign keys) Enforcements help keep your data consistent and accurate. Be aware of any restrictions when modifying data.

- **Transactions:** Especially when performing many changes, consider wrapping your SQL statements in a transaction. Transactions allow you to roll back modifications if issues arise. (invalid URL removed([invalid%20URL%20removed]))
- **Logging/Auditing:** For critical data, implement a system to log changes. This aids troubleshooting and allows tracing past actions.

Example Use Case

You manage an online store's database:

1. **Adding a New Product**

```
INSERT INTO products (product_name, description,
price, stock)
VALUES ('Wireless Headphones',
'Noise-canceling...', 149.99, 20);
```

2. **Customer Updates Shipping Address**

```
UPDATE customers
SET shipping_address = '123 Main Street, Anytown'
WHERE customer_id = 105;
```

3. **Marking Unavailable Items**

```
UPDATE products
SET in_stock = 'N'
WHERE stock = 0;
```

Additional Resources

- **Referential Integrity & Foreign Keys:** Explore advanced database design concepts that protect your data's

consistency
(https://www.w3schools.com/sql/sql_foreignkey.asp)

Inserting and Modifying Data: Advanced Approaches

In the previous chapter, you mastered the essentials of data manipulation. Now, we'll tackle more complex scenarios, optimization techniques, and approaches for handling tricky situations.

Advanced Insertion Techniques

- **Bulk Inserts:**
  - **Database Specific Methods:** Explore features for your particular SQL database (e.g., "BULK INSERT" in SQL Server, "COPY" in PostgreSQL) designed for fast loading of large amounts data.
  - **Loading from a File:** Many SQL tools allow direct import from delimited files (CSV, TSV).
- **Inserting from Complex Queries:**
  - **JOINs in INSERT:** Build new rows that draw combined data from existing tables in a single operation.
  - **Calculated Values:** Insert results of computations and function calls directly.

Sophisticated Updates

- **Updates Across Multiple Tables:**

```
UPDATE products p
JOIN product_stock ps ON p.product_id =
ps.product_id
SET p.price = p.price * 1.05, -- Increase price
    ps.stock = ps.stock - 5    -- Decrease stock
WHERE ...;
```

- **Correlated Subqueries:** Update rows based on values calculated from related rows or tables. These updates often involve aggregation (SUM, AVG).
- **Triggers:** Create "rules" on your database, performing automated updates or insertions in response to certain events (another row being changed, etc.).

Data Modification Best Practices

- **Temporary Tables:** For complex transformations with intermediary steps, temporarily storing calculations (and even restructured data) can improve readability and make debugging easier.
- **Testing and Validation:** In a test environment, verify the impact and correctness of your updates and inserts *before* executing on live data.
- **Performance:** For very large tables, techniques like indexing become crucial to efficient updates.

Beyond the Basics

- **Upserts:** ("Update or Insert"): If a matching row already exists, it's updated. If not, a new row is inserted. Your database may have specific syntax for this (e.g., "ON DUPLICATE KEY UPDATE" in MySQL).
- **Versioning and "Soft Deletes":** For sensitive data, instead of deletion, mark a row as inactive. Implement features to view (or optionally undo) past changes when needed.

Example: Inventory Management

Imagine updating your product inventory system:

1. **Shipment of New Stock (Bulk):** Bulk load from a CSV file provided by your supplier.
2. **Price Adjustment After Promotion:**

```
UPDATE products
SET price = price * 0.85 -- 15% discount
WHERE product_id IN (SELECT product_id FROM
promotion_items);
```

3. **Trigger for Low Stock Warning:** Automatically triggers an email notification when a product's stock level falls below a threshold.

Additional Resources

- **Stored Procedures:** Create reusable blocks of SQL code encapsulating complex updates or insertions https://dev.mysql.com/doc/refman/8.0/en/stored-programs-defining.html
- **CDC (Change Data Capture):** Track historical changes to your data, often used for data warehousing and integration purposes https://www.percona.com/blog/2020/06/02/how-to-set-up-mysql-change-data-capture/

Challenge yourself by coming up with your own complex modification scenarios. Don't hesitate to experiment within a test database environment.

Conclusion

Congratulations! You've covered a tremendous amount of ground. From the foundations of databases to sophisticated data transformations and modifications, you have a powerful SQL toolkit at your disposal. But here's the secret: your SQL journey is far from over.

Staying Current, Staying Engaged

SQL, like any technology, evolves. Here's how to stay sharp and inspired:

- **Practice, Practice, Practice:** Seek out online challenges, small projects, or analyze datasets relevant to your hobbies or job. Consistent practice strengthens your skills.
- **Explore Database-Specific Extensions:** Your chosen SQL flavor likely offers specialized functions and syntax beyond the fundamentals. Research these add-ons to maximize efficiency and effectiveness.
- **Connect with the Community:** Online forums, Q&A sites, and user groups are full of fellow SQL learners and experts. Share knowledge, discuss challenges, and keep yourself engaged and supported.

The Power of SQL in Action

Data in today's world shapes trends, decisions, and innovation. The ability to confidently query, analyze and shape data using SQL empowers you in these areas:

- **Business Insights:** Dive deep into sales trends, customer behavior, or optimize operational processes.
- **Scientific Research:** Manage experimental data and power statistical analysis.

- **Web Development:** Seamlessly integrate SQL with backend and frontend logic for dynamic applications.
- **Personal Projects:** Explore anything from budget analysis to tracking sports statistics. SQL can make sense of the numbers around you.

Closing Thoughts

Remember, SQL is a continuous learning process. With every dataset, every new function, and every complex query you unravel, your proficiency strengthens. Don't shy away from challenging problems; that's where real growth happens.

The power of SQL is the power to harness information. Utilize your newfound skills to unlock insights, make informed decisions, and turn raw data into tangible value!

Thank you for joining me on this guide to SQL basics. Go forth and explore the data-driven world with confidence!